SUPER SKILLS

HOW TO CREATE ANIMATION

IN 10 EASY LESSONS

WILLIAM BISHOP-STEPHENS

QED

Quarto is the authority on a wide range of topics.

Quarto educates, entertains and enriches the lives of our readers—enthusiasts and lovers of hands-on living

www.quartoknows.com

ABOUT THE AUTHOR

Will Bishop-Stephens is a freelance animation director and writer as well as a lecturer at the University of East London and previously the Royal College of Art. He's worked on a number of animation projects and has showcased work at international film festivals. Will has 14 years' experience leading animation workshops for children and young people.

Copyright © Marshall Editions 2016

First published in the UK in 2016 by
QED Publishing
Part of The Quarto Group
The Old Brewery
6 Blundell Street
London N7 9BH

A catalogue record for this book is available from the British Library.

ISBN: 978-1-78493-609-9

Printed in China

Publisher: Maxime Boucknooghe
Art Director: Susi Martin
Editorial Director: Laura Knowles
Design: Kevin Knight
Original illustrations: Joanna Kerr

CONTENTS

SO YOU WANT TO BE AN ANIMATOR?

Animation is amazing! You can bring movement to beautiful, detailed drawings or make two blobs of modelling clay fight each other. You can piece together a disaster movie starring your favourite toys, or even make your best friend vanish. Anything you can imagine, you can animate! In this book you will discover 10 skills you need to become an expert animator. And before you know it, you'll be making everything from two-dimensional fairytales to three-dimensional sci-fi epics!

WHAT IS ANIMATION?

Animation is the trick of bringing something to life with the illusion of movement. The illusion is created when a series of still images, which are only slightly different from each other, are flashed before your eyes. Your brain then sees this series as one moving image.

WHAT YOU NEED:

To turn an animation into a moving image on a screen, you'll need a smartphone, a tablet, or a computer or laptop with a webcam or a digital camera. You'll also need some animation software.

WHAT SOFTWARE SHOULD I CHOOSE?

There are lots of free and affordable animation software available. Type 'stop motion' into your app store to access a free or low-cost animation app. All you need from the app is a function called 'onion-skinning', which will allow you to arrange a series of still images into a sequence, and a feature to play back your animation.

ALWAYS ASK FOR PERMISSION FROM AN ADULT BEFORE YOU BUY OR DOWNLOAD ANYTHING FROM THE INTERNET.

SOFTWARE BASICS

FRAME RATE

When you open your software app, it may ask you what 'frame rate' you want to use. This is the speed the software is going to play back the images (each still image is called a frame).

The frame rate is measured in 'frames per second', or 'fps'.

For example, to make one second of an animation at 12 fps, you would need to create 12 frames. Most stop motion animation is captured at 12 frames per second.

ONION SKINNING

When you've captured a frame, you will see a live view of what's in front of the camera, and a ghost image of the previous frame. This is to help you line up your frame with the previous one. This feature is often called 'onion skinning', after the transparent skins of an onion.

TIMELINE

The 'timeline' is a sequence of images that makes up the animation. It usually allows you to delete or duplicate an individual frame.

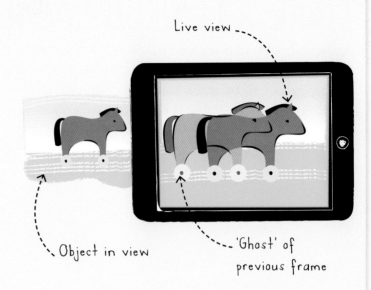

Live view

Object in view

'Ghost' of previous frame

In many apps, you can tap the camera icon in the top right-hand corner to go back to animating.

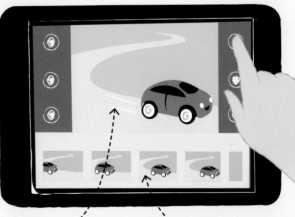

Frame

Timeline

DON'T PANIC!

If this all sounds too complicated, don't worry! You will find out more about editing software on page 56. You can also find definitions of technical and unfamiliar terms in the Glossary on page 63. By the end of the book you'll be able to amaze your friends and family with your very own short animated films.

HANDY TIP!
Apps have helpful videos and tutorials online that show you how to use their features.

MAKE A FLICKBOOK LOOP

The first animation most beginners make is with a flickbook, also known as a flipbook. For example, they may draw on the edge of an exercise book a teacher falling off a cliff or becoming a flying superhero and then riffle the pages to animate the action. In this Super Skill, you will learn how to create a flickbook, photograph and animate it. You will then loop it so it plays for ever and ever. It's the simplest form of digital animation!

GETTING STARTED

All you need is a set of pages that can be 'riffled' (flicked up and released quickly) with your thumb. On each page of your flickbook you draw an image. When you riffle the pages, each image is replaced by the next almost as soon as you see it, and this creates the illusion of movement.

If you have a small notebook or a pack of sticky notes, you can start right away on page 8. If you only have a sheet of A4 paper, you can find out how to make a flickbook on the opposite page.

'WOW' FACTOR!

SOME OF THE FIRST MOVIES EVER MADE WERE SEQUENCES OF IMAGES ON STIFF CARD MOUNTED ON A BIG WHEEL. YOU TURNED A HANDLE TO FLICK EACH IMAGE AND WATCHED IT AS IT WENT PAST A VIEWING HOLE. ONE SUCH MACHINE TO APPEAR IN AMERICA WAS THE 'NICKELODEON' (NICKEL THEATRE). PEOPLE HAD TO PAY A NICKEL (A COIN LIKE A PENNY) TO TURN THE HANDLE AND WATCH THE IMAGE MOVE.

WHAT YOU NEED:

- Plain A4 paper
- Small bulldog clip or stapler
- Scissors
- Coloured pens
- A creative brain

HOW TO MAKE A 16-FRAME FLICKBOOK

To make a flickbook from a sheet of paper:

1. Take a sheet of plain A4 paper.

2. Fold it neatly in half, along its longer side.

3. Fold it again, along its longer side.

4. Fold it once again, along its longer sides.

5. Fold it yet again, along its longer side. (Yes, that's four folds!)

6. Use a bulldog clip or stapler to fasten the folded paper together on one of the shorter sides.

7. Use large scissors to cut through the folds on the remaining three sides. You might need some adult help with this.

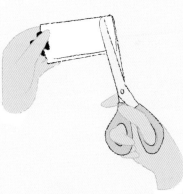

Fold along the long side, four times

Clip or staple the short edge

Cut off the folds on the other three sides

HANDY TIP!

One of the best ways to flick is to hold the clipped edge of the flip book in your hand. Press the other side of the book against your thumb so the book is bending, and flip the pages away from your thumb, a page at a time.

DON'T WORRY IF IT'S WONKY!

You should be able to riffle or flick through the pages smoothly from back to front. You might need to flatten the edges of the pages so that they don't catch and jump several frames of your animation. If it is still a bit wonky and skips pages when you flip through it, don't worry. When you photograph the pages to make the frames of your animation, you can hold each page open in turn. The app will create the movement. Now turn over to learn how to draw and capture the frames.

DRAWING AND PHOTOGRAPHING YOUR FRAMES

Once you have your empty pages, you are ready to start drawing the frames of your animation. You will draw a different step of the action on each page to form the frames. So what do you draw that will make a great animation? This is where your creative brain comes in to play!

IDEAS FOR YOUR FIRST ANIMATION

- A stick person walking up stairs
- A bee landing on a flower
- A flying saucer vaporising a planet
- A windmill turning
- An anvil falling on a person's head
- A person biting an apple

HANDY TIP!

Go wild! The wackiest ideas are often the best. If something doesn't work, think of it as good practice and try another one.

ANIMATORS HAVE A SAYING: "THE MAGIC HAPPENS BETWEEN THE FRAMES". THIS IS BECAUSE OUR BRAINS FILL IN ALL THE ACTION BETWEEN EACH STILL IMAGE TO MAKE A FLOW OF MOVEMENT THAT ISN'T REALLY THERE.

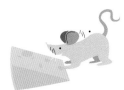

Tip 1: START AT THE BACK

Draw your first frame on the inside back page using a dark-coloured pen or pencil. Trace your next drawing on the page above making a tiny change in the movement, and then a third drawing above that with another small change, and keep going until you complete the action.

Tip 3: KEEP IT SIMPLE

Small, complicated actions can be difficult to make out and may confuse the brain, so make your drawings bold and the movement clear and simple.

Tip 2: SMOOTH CHANGES

Make sure each drawing is similar enough to the previous one to trick your brain into seeing smooth movement when you play back the animation.

Tip 4: CHECK YOUR SPEED

Test your animation every few frames by riffling. You'll soon become good at judging how small the changes need to be in order to make the movement smooth and believable. If the movement is too fast, you need to break the action down into smaller parts to make more frames. If the movement is too slow, you need to complete the action in fewer frames.

HANDY TIP!
You can change the settings of many cameras to show guidelines or grids in the viewfinder, to help you position the pages in the same place.

PHOTOGRAPHING YOUR FRAMES

Now it's time to photograph each page of the flickbook using your animation software. Photograph the pages in sequence so that the back page (the beginning of your animation) becomes frame 01, the next page becomes frame 02, the next 03, and so on. To keep the book open, either break the book apart and lay each page flat, or hold it open with your hand.

Keep your hand in the same place in each frame so that only the drawings appear to move between frames. You don't need to hold the camera completely still between images: you can use the software's onion skinning to line up the images.

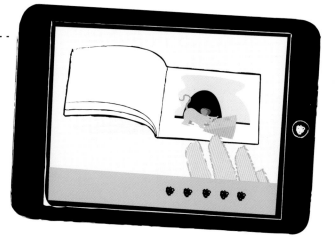

Photograph the pages of your flickbook on a plain, uncluttered surface. That way, when the animation is played, the background will remain still and not interfere with the action.

PLAYING THE MOVIE

It feels magical when you use the animation app to make your flickbook flick by itself. When you play back the animation, the drawings are literally moving next to your hand! Don't worry if you don't get it right first time, just look at what went wrong, correct the error and record the action again. You need to be willing to make lots of versions and learn from your mistakes. Practice really does make perfect!

Tip 1: TRY DIFFERENT FRAME RATES

Try changing the speed of your animation by altering the frame rate. Remember, 12 fps is a good number for achieving smooth movement. If you drop below 8 fps, you'll start to see the separate images, not flowing movement, and the illusion will not work.

Making the moves too big between frames is the most common mistake new animators make, ending up with a 'jumping' effect. If the action is playing back too fast, make smaller moves per frame to slow it down. You will need more frames to complete the action.

Tip 2: SETTING THE RESOLUTION

Resolution is a way of describing the size of your movie. This is usually measured in pixels, which refers to the number of tiny squares of colour that makes up your image on the screen. If it's possible, set your animation to a High Definition size, such as 1920 x 1080, sometimes written as 'HD 1080p'. A movie will appear horribly blocky if you scale it up from a low to a high resolution, but it is fine to play a high-resolution movie at a smaller size.

HANDY TIP!
For each new project, you'll need to set up a new file in your software. If you don't, all your animations will stack up in the same movie.

LOOP IT!

Did you know you can make your animation run forever by creating a loop? A loop is where you end your animation with the same frame you started with. Once you set it to repeat, during play back it will jump from the last frame back to the first and keep playing.

Most apps automatically loop your animation when you hit the 'Play' button. You can also copy and paste all your frames to make them repeat as many times as you like. In some apps you can also use 'reverse selected frames' to make the action run backwards. This is great if you want to create an action such as a character bowing: you can bend them forwards frame by frame, and then copy and reverse the frames to make them stand up again.

TRY THIS!

◦ Make a flickbook with a looping action. Start with a circle on frame 01 and end with a circle on frame 16.

◦ Make slight changes to your circle; over 10 frames mutate it frame by frame into a strange creature, lovely flower or alien spaceship.

◦ Change it back into a circle in the last six frames.

◦ The circle in the final frame should be identical to the circle you began with in frame 01, to complete the loop.

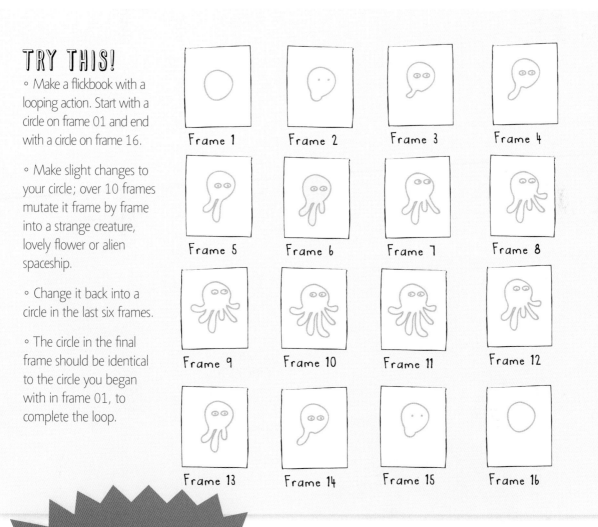

Frame 1 Frame 2 Frame 3 Frame 4
Frame 5 Frame 6 Frame 7 Frame 8
Frame 9 Frame 10 Frame 11 Frame 12
Frame 13 Frame 14 Frame 15 Frame 16

YOU WILL BE AT YOUR MOST CREATIVE WHEN YOU'RE HAVING FUN WITH ANIMATION. SMILE, RELAX AND START PLAYING WITH YOUR IDEAS!

CONGRATULATIONS!

You have now learnt the basics of how to create an animation. Everything else builds on this, so let's move onto the next Super Skill.

PIXILATION

A great way to make quick stop motion animation is to use other people (or even yourself if no one else is around) as props and characters. You can make a friend glide on an invisible skateboard, drive an invisible car or even hover above the ground. It really is fun!

GLIDING ON AN INVISIBLE SKATEBOARD

Are you ready to make an animation of a friend on an invisible skateboard? The technique you will use is called pixilation. It involves taking a frame of a live actor – your friend – before you move them to a slightly different position and take a new frame. You move them again and take another frame, and so on until you complete the action.

GETTING STARTED

Find a clear area to film in. If you don't have a friend nearby to film, prop up the camera so its viewfinder captures the whole of the area you will be moving in. Set the camera software to 'time lapse' or 'timer', so it will take a frame at regular intervals, then move into position for frame 01.

PIXILATION IS NAMED AFTER THE MAGICAL LITTLE PIXIES OF FOLKLORE. BECAUSE THE EFFECT LOOKS LIKE MAGIC! IT HAS NOTHING TO DO WITH PIXELS.

MAKING THE FRAMES

∘ Stand as if you're on a skateboard and take frame 1.

∘ Keeping your arms and legs in the same position, shuffle forwards a few centimetres. Take frame 02.

∘ Next, move twice as much as you did last time and take frame 03. This will give the effect of speeding up. (You will find out more about speeding up and slowing down on pages 14–15.)

∘ Keep adding frames, moving more each time, until you are moving the width of your body. If you're filming a friend, you can make them go around the room and around obstacles. If your camera is fixed, they will have to stay in view of your camera.

∘ You could end your movie by filming them going through a doorway. An even more dramatic end might be to have them go through a wall! Capture them approaching the wall a frame at a time. Once they reach the wall, move them out of shot and take several frames of the empty space.

∘ Every 12 pictures you take will give you one second of animation (remember "12 fps"). So if you want to whiz around the room for a couple of seconds you will need to take 24 frames and for four seconds you will need 48 frames.

TRY THIS!

When you've got the hang of filming your friend skateboarding, try filming them ice skating or performing any other crazy move you can think up. Pixilation can even be used to combine live action and animated models in one movie!

HANDY TIP!

Some apps tend to play movies at 5 fps, so the action looks jerky and slow. Remember to change the setting to 12 fps. You may need to do this regularly.

SMOOTHNESS AND FLOW

So you have amazed friends with your mastery of pixilation! But how can you slow down and speed up the action, and keep nice flows of movement? In this section we will look at the clever methods you can use to create all kinds of smooth movement.

Tip 1: SLOW ACTION

Smaller moves per frame equals slower action. If you want to film your friend skating slowly you'll need to get them to move tiny amounts per frame, so the onion skin image of the previous frame almost completely overlaps the new image.

Tip 2: FAST ACTION

Larger moves between frames equals faster action. How big you make the move depends on the type of action. For example, you can capture a jump or a punch in three frames: frame one shows the person getting ready to perform the action, the second catches the action in full flow and the final frame shows the end point of the action.

Most fast moves need to last longer than three frames. When animating invisible skateboarding, for example, the skateboarder's body in each frame should be just in front of the onion skin image. The nose on the onion skin should be touching the back of the live-image head. If the move between frames is too big, your brain will stop linking up the images and the animation will appear jerky.

THINGS TO TRY

FLYING!

Ask your friend to jump on the spot and take a frame. Repeat this lots of times, then play back the animation and, if done correctly, you will see them hovering. You need to be patient – it's hard to capture the millisecond when both their feet are completely off the floor.

Tip 3: SMOOTH MOVEMENT

Maintaining steady changes and a consistent line of motion equals smooth movement. The diagrams below show that smooth action depends on keeping smooth changes between each frame and staying true to the line of the movement. If you make small moves and big moves at random, or go off the natural line of the motion, you end up with jerky animation.

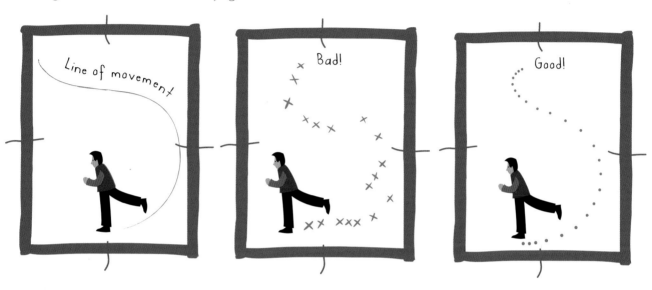

Tip 4: ADJUSTING FRAMES PER SECOND

While it's true that a lot of animators work at 12 fps, for creating really smooth movement, you could go as high as 24 fps and make really small changes between each frame. This will slow down the action, of course.

For speeding up the movement, you could play the action at 5 fps. But do bear in mind that at this speed the animation will stop looking like realistic movement and more more like a fast slide show.

INVISIBLE CAR!

Ask your friend to sit on a chair in a driving position, holding an invisible steering wheel and with their feet on invisible pedals. Move the chair towards the camera frame by frame, but make sure your friend stays in the same position. Start with small forward moves and increase them steadily to accelerate your car. You could have your friend 'crash' into the camera for a dramatic finale.

GET THINGS MOVING

Now that you've learnt how to capture an action frame by frame, you're ready to animate all sorts of things. You can move objects as if by magic or bring toys to life. Anything that will hold a pose can be animated. This sort of animation is known as stop motion.

TRY THIS!

To get to grips with stop motion, set up a small group of objects on a tabletop and follow these steps to gradually bring them to life.

1 Take a few frames of the still objects. This will set the scene.

2 Now move one object by a small amount and capture the frame.

3 Move it a small amount again and capture the next frame.

4 Continue making small moves with your object, taking individual frames that build up the motion, just like you did with the pixilation task.

5 Slow down movements by breaking them down into several frames, but complete fast movements in one or two frames, to give them more punch.

6 Once you are confident, start moving a second object at the same time, then add a third, and so on. Soon you'll have a host of dancing objects!

WHAT YOU NEED:

- Ordinary objects or toys
- A camera, smartphone or tablet
- A clear tabletop or desk

FIRST ATTEMPTS

While you're learning the technique, don't worry about creating a story or a set. Have fun experimenting with making objects come to life. As your skills improve you will be able to add character to toys and everyday objects.

Keep the first movies you make short and simple. That way you will spot your mistakes before you've spent too much time setting things up and taking lots of frames. You'll soon get a better feel for timing and spacing, and your animations will improve.

YOU WILL LEARN AS MUCH BY GETTING THINGS WRONG AS GETTING THINGS RIGHT!

WOAH, STEADY DOES IT!

Make sure your camera does not move when you press the button to capture a frame. If you don't have a stand, use a blob of modelling clay to hold it in place or tape it to a mug or box with masking tape. Look through the viewfinder to make sure that the prop isn't obscuring any part of the camera lens on your device.

HANDY TIP!
Make a habit of taking video or photos of anything that might be useful for animation. Write down your ideas in a notebook or the equivalent on your phone app so that you don't forget them.

ANIMATING TOYS

Do you have an action figure with limbs you can move into different positions? If so, you have a ready-made character to star in your stop-motion shoot. But now you also have more complicated actions to think about.

A FAST COMEDY WADDLE

A toy figure with jointed arms and legs makes a great animation puppet! Start by animating your toy waddling along until you feel confident about lifting its legs to shoot a more elegant walk. To make the figure waddle, move one of its legs forwards as if it's taking a stride and capture the frame. Then bring the second leg forwards to meet the first and take another frame. Repeat this several times and you will see a fast comedy waddle when you play back the animation.

'WOW' FACTOR!

A LITTLE BIT OF STICKY TACK UNDER THE FOOT OF A CHARACTER MAKES IT HARDER TO ACCIDENTLY KNOCK THEM OVER, AND IT ALSO MEANS YOU CAN MAKE THEM WALK UP VERTICAL SURFACES!

HANDY TIP!

Search car boot sales or charity shops for toys to use in your movies. You'll find lots of cheap and unusual things!

ARMS AND LEGS

Have you ever paid close attention to how a person walks? Notice how their arms move to balance the movement of their legs. The strip below shows nine stages of arms-and-legs movement you can copy, frame by frame, to animate your toy figure. Repeat the sequence from stages 1 to 9 to produce a smooth walk.

STEP 1
Start with the figure standing still, with arms by its sides.

STEP 2
Lift the right leg and left arm forwards. Move the right arm back a little. The figure is still standing straight up.

STEP 3
Make the figure lean over a little, so the right foot moves forwards and down. The left foot starts to lift and the left leg bends backwards.

STEP 4
Place the right foot on the floor, with the left foot lifting almost off the floor. The left leg is now bent back and the figure is almost standing upright again.

STEP 5
Move the figure forwards to the standing position, with both arms by its sides.

STEP 6
Lift the left leg and right arm forwards. Move the left arm back a little. The figure is still standing upright.

STEP 7
Make the figure lean forwards a little, so the left foot moves forwards and down a little. The right foot starts to lift and the leg bends backwards

STEP 8
Place the left foot on the floor, with the right foot lifting almost off the floor. The right leg is now bent back and the figure is again almost upright.

STEP 9
Move the figure forwards to the standing position, with both arms by its sides.

HANDY TIP!
Don't forget to use the onion skinning feature of your animation software!

STORYBOARDS AND SHOTS

Once you're confident you can move your models the way you want to capture the frames, you can start planning longer shots and stories. A shot is all the animation you shoot within a single setting while keeping the camera on the same spot. You can create a story by putting the shots together.

WHAT MAKES A STORY?

Often there are three parts to a story:

○ **The beginning**. This is where we meet a character for the first time and find out about them: 'Once there was a knight who stomped about shouting orders at people.'

○ **The conflict**. This is where the character is faced with a problem: 'The knight was out riding when he met a giant troll blocking his path. He shouted at the troll, but the troll ignored him. It just sniffled and kept looking at one of its own feet.'

○ **The resolution**. This is where the character acts to resolve the problem: 'The knight noticed that the troll had a big thorn stuck in the bottom of his foot. He pulled the thorn out. The troll smiled and moved out of the way.'

Tip 1: CREATE A STORYBOARD

A storyboard is a great visual device to plan your story on paper. It is like a cartoon strip showing all the shots you'd like to film. It enables you to plan long action sequences, prepare all the things you need and also spot any problems before you begin.

A storyboard isn't meant to show every single frame of your story. It might show just one panel for each shot, or a few panels if it's a shot with a lot of action in it. A storyboard gives an overview of what happens in your story from start to finish.

YOUR STORYBOARD SHOULD TELL YOU:

○ Who the characters are

○ What they are doing

○ Where they end up

○ How they get there

Title ....

Director/s ....

Page number .....   Date ....

Tip 2: PLAN AMAZING SHOTS

Here are some shots you can use to make your animations look exciting and professional.

EXTREME CLOSE-UP

This is the most zoomed-in shot, usually on a character, and creates a dramatic effect. You can use it to show a character's emotions because their face fills the entire frame.

CLOSE-UP

In this shot, you can see some of the character's gestures, such as a shrug of their shoulders, but not much of the their surroundings.

MID SHOT

This shot shows a character's upper body and their surroundings, and can fit two characters with ease. This is a 'normal' shot used for a lot of the storytelling in most films, when characters are engaged in conversation.

OVER-THE-SHOULDER SHOT

This is a good way to show a conversation from a character's point of view. You only see the back of their head and one shoulder; the shot gives viewers a sense that they are seeing the world through a character's eyes.

LONG SHOT

A long shot shows the whole character, the way they are standing and any action that's happening around them.

EXTREME LONG SHOT

Here the camera is much further away. The viewer can see the landscape the character is in. It is a shot commonly used to establish where a character is, what is around them and whether they are alone or with people.

CLAYMATION

In this chapter, you're going to get to grips with one of the most fun and effective types of animation for any budding animator – claymation.

Modelling clay: the animator's enemy!

"Modelling clay is terrible stuff. It droops and falls over and changes shape. All the colours get mixed up and bits of fluff always get stuck in it."

Modelling clay is the animator's friend!

"It's brilliant stuff that bends and squashes and stays where you put it. It comes in all different colours and never dries out. You can sculpt beautiful models out of it that... oh no! It's stuck to the table!"

In fact, both these opinions of modelling clay are true. But keep in mind that some of the best animated films have been made with the material, so it must be worth the trouble. The top tips in this chapter will teach you the skills to make the most of modelling clay.

MAKE SURE YOU HAVE THE RIGHT STUFF!

The first step to successful claymation is making sure you are using the right type of clay.

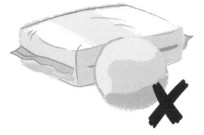

Air-dry clay and ceramic clay will dry out and become crumbly. Don't try to use them for animation.

Oven-baked polymer clays such as Fimo® aren't as easy to mould and bend, even before they are baked.

HANDY TIP!
When you make your first few claymation characters, keep them bold and simple. If you spend lots of time making fiddly, detailed characters, you might find they fall apart when you make your film. As you gain experience, experiment with more detailed models.

Playdough isn't the same as modelling clay – it's more springy and doesn't hold its shape as well.

Modelling clay such as Plasticine™ is the ideal material for claymation. You can buy it in big 500g blocks in art shops. It's not as squishy as the flat packs you can find in toy shops, so it holds its shape better. It's also better value for money.

For clean colours, get the **single colour packs**. Blue and black will come off onto your fingers, so it's a good idea to have some wet wipes handy on set, to stop your fingers making the other colours dirty.

WHILE YOU'RE LEARNING HOW TO USE MODELLING CLAY, KEEP IT SIMPLE. DON'T BE TOO AMBITIOUS ABOUT THE MODELS YOU CREATE. YOUR SKILLS WILL IMPROVE WITH PRACTISE.

WHAT'S IT GOING TO LOOK LIKE?

It can be tempting to spend lots of time using your modelling clay to create a wonderfully detailed character for your animation. However, it's better to start practising your claymation skills with a small ball of modelling clay, rather than spend a whole day making a lovely model that breaks apart the moment you try to move it. Here are two easy exercises to get you started.

To create your set, all you need is a sheet of white A3 paper. Prop the sheet up into a curved shape using a box, books or a pile of magazines, as shown in the image below.

Position your camera, tablet or smartphone so that the lens has a clear view of your paper set.

Roll your blob of modelling clay into a smooth, round ball and place it in the centre of your paper.

WHAT YOU NEED:

- A blob of modelling clay big enough to roll into the size of a soft ball.
- A sheet of white A3 paper
- Sticky tape
- A box or some books to prop up the sheet of paper
- A camera, or equivalent on a laptop, phone or tablet.

HANDY TIP!

Make sure your set is positioned at a good height in relation to your camera. The camera angle should be high enough so that you can see the paper floor but none of the edges, and you shouldn't be looking directly down on the ball of modelling clay.

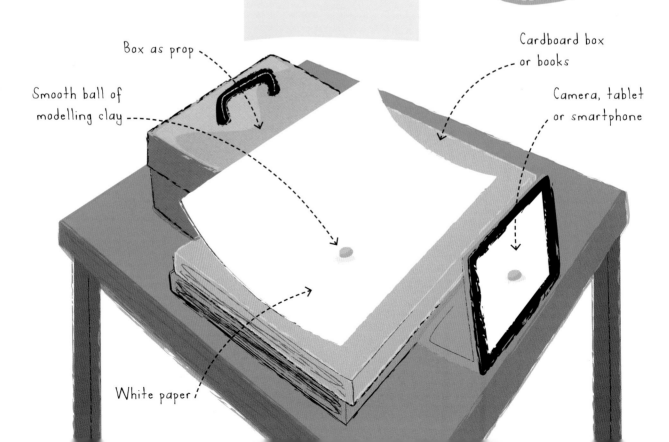

Box as prop

Smooth ball of modelling clay

Cardboard box or books

Camera, tablet or smartphone

White paper

Exercise 1: THE 'SQUASH AND STRETCH'

Now you're ready to bring your blob of modelling clay to life! The image in the camera's viewfinder should look something like frame number 1.

Take a series of six photos, moulding your ball of modelling clay into different shapes each time, as shown here.

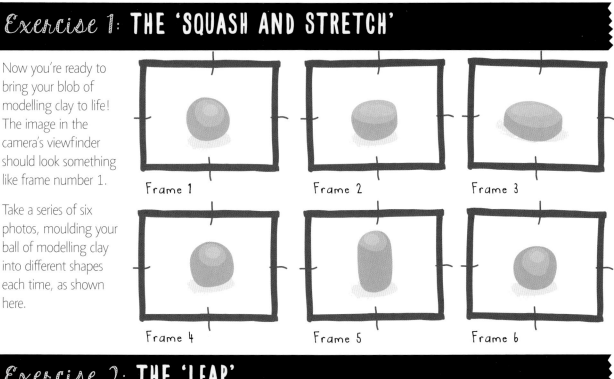

Frame 1

Frame 2

Frame 3

Frame 4

Frame 5

Frame 6

Exercise 2: THE 'LEAP'

Once you have the hang of the 'squash and stretch' technique, try animating your blob of modelling clay 'leaping'. Take six more photos of your blob, this time moulded into the shapes shown here.

Now, when you play back these series of photos quickly, you will see that the blob appears to be moving! This is the basis for all claymation, it's just that the more ambitious your model and the movement you wish to create, the more time and effort it will take to animate.

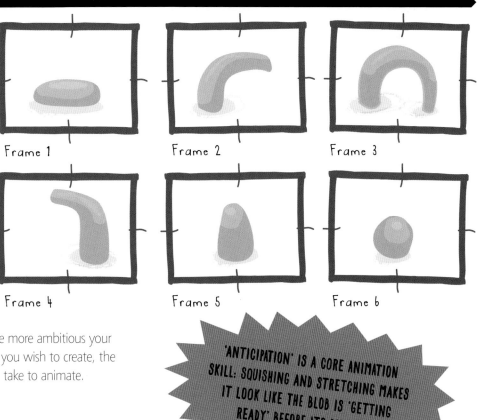

Frame 1

Frame 2

Frame 3

Frame 4

Frame 5

Frame 6

'ANTICIPATION' IS A CORE ANIMATION SKILL: SQUISHING AND STRETCHING MAKES IT LOOK LIKE THE BLOB IS 'GETTING READY' BEFORE ITS BIG LEAP.

MAKING A CLAYMATION CHARACTER

The ability to make a claymation character whose arms and head don't fall off when you move them is a very important skill for animation. It's easy to do when you know how.

WHAT YOU NEED:

- Three or more colours of modelling clay (not white)
- Small white acrylic beads (alternatively, you can use white clay instead of the beads)
- A clay modelling tool

BODY

First, mould the shape of a hollow body by wrapping a blob of modelling clay around your thumb. Flare out the end slightly to make a bell shape, so its fits over the legs.

LEGS

Roll some modelling clay to make a long sausage shape about the thickness of your thumb, and bend it at the middle to form the legs. Fit the body over the legs.

HANDY TIP!

Make the body and legs quite chunky. A puppet that's too tall can be wobbly to animate. For a character who is going to move around a lot, it's best to make them short and stocky.

NECK

Roll a bit of clay to make the neck. Then use the thin end of a modelling tool to carve a hole in the top of the body and push the neck into the hole.

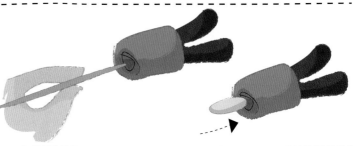

HEAD AND FACE

Roll some clay into a flat disk for the head and push two beads into disk for the eyes. Add tiny strips of clay to make the eyebrows and a different-coloured blob for the nose. Use your modelling tool to carve a mouth-shaped hole and make another hole for the neck. Connect the head to the neck.

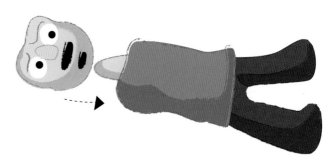

'WOW' FACTOR!

YOU CAN CREATE DIFFERENT SHADES OF MODELLING CLAY BY BLENDING COLOURS TOGETHER, AS YOU CAN WITH PAINT. YOU COULD MAKE YOUR CHARACTER'S EARS AND NOSE SLIGHTLY REDDER IN TONE FOR A MORE REALISTIC EFFECT. YOU CAN EVEN MAKE THESE FEATURES BRIGHT RED TO ACHIEVE A FUNNIER LOOK.

AS YOU BECOME MORE SKILLED, YOU CAN CHANGE THE SHAPE OF THE MOUTH AS YOU ANIMATE YOUR CHARACTER.

ARMS, THE WRONG WAY!

Most people attach the arms by hanging them on the side of the body... only for the arms to fall off when they lift them up!

ARMS, THE RIGHT WAY!

The right way to fit an arm, so it stays on when you move it, is to smear the end of the arm onto the body, pressing it down all the way round, as shown here.

THE FINISHED CHARACTER

Ta-daa! Your moveable figure is complete! He is now ready to star in your animation. You should be able to move his arms, legs and neck without him falling apart. Don't be rough, though!

WHEN SHOULD YOU USE WIRE?

With a big character, you might need to use pipe-cleaner wire to strengthen the limbs. The fur on the wire helps keep it from poking through the modelling clay.

If you struggle to keep your character upright, build your puppet around a length of pipe-cleaner wire that goes from the top of the head and down one leg to a loop of wire in the foot. You can pin the loop down with a drawing pin.

THINK BIG, BUILD SMALL

Now that you know how to animate a range of objects and characters, it's time to think about your backgrounds. In this Super Skill we'll look at where to work and how you can create hills and forests – in short, how to fake scale and make your characters, objects and setting appear life size!

WHERE TO SET UP

Here are some tips that are relevant to all sorts of stop motion animation.

° A good place to set up your camera is where there aren't people or pets milling about, so they won't accidentally knock your models over or cast shadows as they walk by.

° Pushing a table or desk against a wall will give you a great starting point for propping up all kinds of background and scenery.

° Choose a place where you can light your scene with artificial light rather than daylight, because slight changes in the weather will appear in your animation as flickering light. A flexible desk lamp is perfect for lighting your scene.

It's frustrating to spend time on an animation and then have it ruined - make sure you find a safe space to leave your project and come back to it.

MAKE YOUR OWN STUDIO

If you are really into animation, a big, stiff cardboard box is just the perfect thing to make into a versatile mini studio. Ideally, find a box about 60 centimetres long on all sides, big enough for an A2 sheet of paper to fit inside. Boxes made from corrugated cardboard are best, because they stay stiff. You will need to cut the top and one side open, as shown below – ask an adult to help you with this.

WHAT YOU NEED:

- Large cardboard box about 60 centimetres long on all sides
- Scissors
- Thick sheet of A1 white paper
- Thick sheets of A2 blue and green paper
- Sheets of multicoloured A4 paper
- Masking tape
- Sticky tack, such as Blu-Tack®

Cut off the top of the box and one side.

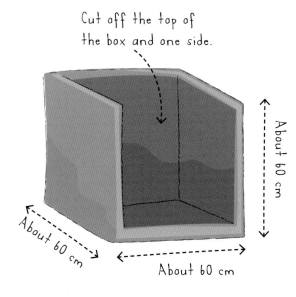

About 60 cm

About 60 cm

About 60 cm

ONCE YOU'VE MADE YOUR BOX, YOU CAN CREATE CHANGEABLE SETS AND USE IT FOR ALL SORTS OF ANIMATION, AS YOU WILL SEE IN THE FOLLOWING PAGES.

BUILDING YOUR SETS

Now you've made your box studio, you're ready to learn the key techniques for making a miniature set. Although you are building on a small scale, you will find that you can cheat the camera to make your characters and props look huge. So it's time to think big!

INFINITY CURVE!

To create a white space that seems to go on forever, use masking tape to hang an A1 sheet of thick white paper along the back of your box and across the floor. Don't push the paper into the back corner. You want it to sit in a gentle curve so the camera doesn't pick up the point where the floor becomes the wall – just like the simple claymation set shown on page 24. When you animate on the floor part of the cardboard mini-studio, it will look like your character is in an infinite, featureless landscape.

'WOW' FACTOR!

AN INFINITY CURVE LOOKS ESPECIALLY GOOD WHEN LIT WITH A STRONG WHITE LIGHT.

HANDY TIP!
Experiment with other colours you can use for landscapes. How about blue for a river or sea, or sandy colour for a desert?

SKY AND HILLS

You can even add a sky and hills and maintain the same sense of an infinite landscape. Hang a sky-blue A2 sheet over the back wall about half way down the curve. Next, lay an A2 sheet of grass-green paper on the box floor about half way up the curve so it overlaps with the sky. Cut the back edge of the green into a wavy line and you have created a huge area of grassland and distant hills. Check out how it looks through the camera.

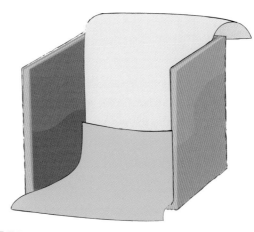

TREES AND HOUSES

Now you can add other features to this landscape such as trees or buildings. Stick a flap of card to the back of each prop to keep it upright and use a tiny pinch of sticky tack to keep it steady on the floor. As you build, keep checking the scene through the camera's viewfinder.

Once you start adding features like trees and houses, you can experiment with scale and distance.

TRY DIFFERENT SIZES

Make three sets of trees that differ in size but are identical shape – small, medium and large.

∘ Place the smallest trees at the back of the scene, adding the next size up a little closer.

∘ Keep looking into your viewfinder to see how the scene appears in your camera.

∘ Build the scene from the back to the front until you have your biggest trees at the front of the scene, closest to the camera.

∘ Do you see how the arrangement of trees gives depth, or perspective, to your scenery? You can use this trick to make your sets appear as big as you like! There are no limits!

IT'S EASIEST TO DRAW AND CUT OUT SIMPLE TREE SHAPES WHILE YOU EXPERIMENT WITH THE SIZES. YOU CAN SPEND TIME ON THEIR SHAPE ONCE YOU KNOW WHAT SIZE YOU NEED.

SMALL FAR AWAY, BIG CLOSE UP

On the previous page you discovered that you can cheat the camera so that your small set looks like a huge landscape. Now that you have a sense of how perspective works, you'll find it useful to divide the set into three spaces for action: the foreground, mid-ground and background. These three spaces aren't something you need to understand to make great animations, but can be used to great effect if you have different-sized versions of the same characters and objects for each of the three spaces.

Foreground

In the foreground, which is the section closest to the camera, your characters fill a big part of the image. So the models you create for this area have to be detailed. A useful advice is to check how much detail your camera will pick up before you start making your model.

You can make your foreground set with folded layers of card, PVA glue and paint on three-dimensional features. When you become more advanced and adventurous, you might want to try foam core card to make your models – foam is a great material both to paint and carve texture into and will give your animation a professional look.

Mid-ground

In the mid-ground, there is less need for detail and texture. Always check what the camera can see before spending hours making something that might be out of focus or hidden by an object in the foreground. If you have action that leaves the foreground and goes back into the mid-ground, you will need to make smaller versions of your characters. That way they can leave the foreground of the shot and a smaller version of them can re-enter the mid-ground, and in doing so appear further away.

Background

Filiming action deep in the scenery can look really convincing. Remember that everything in the background is small enough that it can be made totally flat. Any characters here will be quite tiny, too.

HANDY TIP!

Mixing painted card buildings with modelling clay people and toy cars can look great – anything goes in stop motion animation!

Background

Mid-ground

Foreground

SPECIAL EFFECTS

You will probably have seen lots of TV shows and films that have amazing special effects. These may have featured scenes in which characters were suddenly surrounded by flames or swept away by a huge wave, or performing an impossible feat such as walk on water or flying into outer space.

EXPLOSIONS

In this section, you will find out about the power of 'replacement animation'. That's swapping one object with a similar object between frames, the same way you swapped one drawing with another drawing to make a flickbook, to create the illusion of movement. However, in replacement animation, the change is sudden and this works brilliantly for creating some special effects such as fires and explosions.

WHAT YOU NEED:

- Toy vehicle
- Coloured paper in fiery colours such as red, orange and yellow, as well as green
- Scissors
- Sticky tack

EXPLODING A TOY VEHICLE

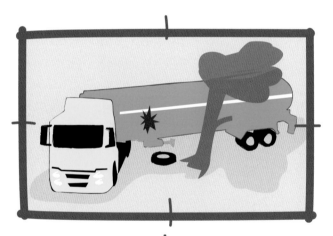

FRAME ONE

Make a small flat explosion shape out of red paper. At the right moment in your movie, for example, when an oil tanker has driven into a tree, attach a small red explosion shape to the source of your explosion. Then capture the frame of animation.

FRAME TWO

Make two larger paper explosion shapes – one in orange and one in yellow. Line up their edges and stick the shapes together to make a two-colour explosion.

Now remove the red explosion shape from the scene. Add the two-colour explosion to the same spot, lining it up using your software's onion-skinning feature. Take frame two.

HANDY TIP!
Don't have an explosion right at the start of a shot. Give your audience about 12 frames to see what's in a scene.

FRAME THREE

Now make three really big explosion shapes: the biggest in yellow, the second biggest in orange and the smallest in red. Make them large enough so that once you stick them together, they hide the vehicle that is exploding. Replace the two-colour explosion with this three-colour explosion. Capture the frame.

FRAME FOUR

Now you need to create the aftermath of the explosion… you will need to show the object blown to pieces, with bits scattered everywhere from the centre of the explosion.

HANDY TIP!

Take several frames of the aftermath so it doesn't end before people get the comic horror impact.

ANIMATING FIRE...

To create a fire effect, make red-, yellow- and orange-coloured flame shapes like those below. Fire sways from side to side and stays roughly the same size.

...AND WATER

Water becomes a puddle when the flow stops. Cut different sizes of the same shape out of blue paper, as shown below. You might need to prop up each card so the water looks more real in the camera. You can grow a puddle frame by frame by replacing each puddle with a larger version.

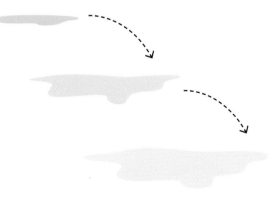

WALK, JUMP, FLY!

Making a wobbly character walk or even stand up is a real problem with model animation. If your model has bendy legs and a big, heavy head, you'll need to hang it from something so it looks as if it is standing. This method also allows you to make your character jump and fly. Whoowee!

A SUPERHERO FLYING RIG

Animators use a device called a 'flying rig' to make characters jump and fly. The flying rig is a pole with two threads dangling from it, on which you hang your model or puppet. For a quick jump that's a couple of frames long, the pole can be supported on a frame, chair or shelf. However, for capturing longer movements such as controlled superhero-style flying, you want a proper rig that fits on your box studio.

HANDY TIP!
You can shade white cotton thread with coloured pens so that it matches your set's background.

WHAT YOU NEED:

- A pole long enough to span the length of your box studio. You could use a tent pole, curtain rod, broom handle or a cardboard tube.
- White cotton thread or thin fishing line
- Two squares of cardboard with a notch cut out
- Two sheets of paper to make pole sleeves
- Scissors
- Masking tape
- Sticky tack
- Soft toy or puppet
- Pins or wire to attach threads to the puppet
- Big sheet of sky-blue paper

The two threads attach to your puppet at the head and waist to create a flying effect.

MAKING THE RIG

1. Wrap two sheets of paper around your pole to make paper sleeves and tape them to keep them from unravelling.

2. The paper sleeves need to fit snuggly on the pole, but also turn freely so you can wind the thread up or down.

3. Attach a thread to each of the paper sleeves with sticky tape, so the threads hang down.

4. Use pins or wire to attach the model to each thread.

5. Tape the two cardboard pole holders to the sides of the box. They will keep the pole in place.

6. If your model is heavy, use extra tape or sticky tack to keep the sleeves from unwinding.

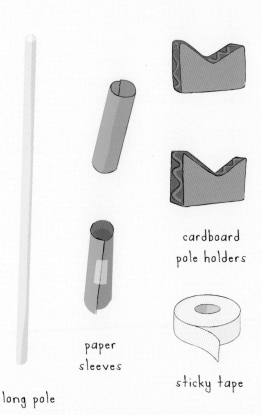

cardboard pole holders

paper sleeves

sticky tape

long pole

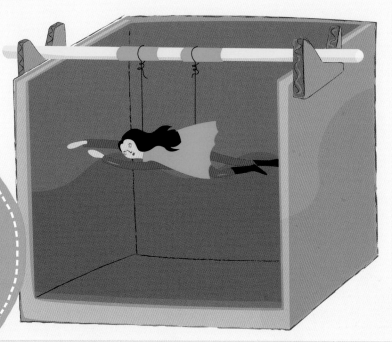

HANDY TIP!
The distance between the threads should be far enough so that your puppet doesn't spin and become tangled up in them. They must also be long enough for you to lower your puppet right down to the ground.

ATTACHING YOUR PUPPET

How you fix your puppet to the threads depends on whether you want it to stand and jump or fly. If you want it to stand or jump, you should push the pins into the puppet's shoulders. If you want to animate it flying, you will need to push one pin into the top of its head and the other into the puppet's bottom.

STANDING AND HOVERING

Now you can raise and lower the two threads by turning the paper sleeves and fixing them at the height you want with sticky tack or masking tape. You'll you need to attach the pins at a high point on the puppet or it will flip over.

With the pins pushed into its shoulders while the puppet is lying down, and with the threads attached to the flying rig (see previous pages) you can wind up the thread until the puppet is standing upright. Wind a little bit more and your character will look like it is jumping, or hovering.

Think back to how you made the blob jump (on page 25), with a crouch right down and a stretch up as you jump. You could even jump around yourself to get a feel for what you do when you jump.

ADVANCED JUMPING!

When you jump up high, you first crouch down a little to power up for the jump. Then you push down on the ground, straighten your legs and jump into the air.

So start by having your character crouch down, over three frames. Unwind the thread so you have enough slack to bend the character's legs. Then straighten the character's legs and wind the character off the ground to almost the top of the jump - remember, it's a sharp explosion of movement! Take the frame. Then raise the character a little more and take another frame. At the top of the jump, the movement slows down. Bring your character halfway down for the next frame. Lower their feet back on the ground for the penultimate frame, with a little bit of a bend in the legs. Finally stand them up for the last frame. Play back the sequence and see how successfully you've animated your character jumping!

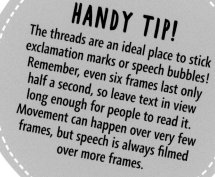

HANDY TIP!

The threads are an ideal place to stick exclamation marks or speech bubbles! Remember, even six frames last only half a second, so leave text in view long enough for people to read it. Movement can happen over very few frames, but speech is always filmed over more frames.

FLYING FREE

To film a puppet moving through the air, put a sky-blue backdrop behind it. Use sticky tack to fix clouds and buildings to the backdrop – you don't need many clouds, because you can reuse them every time they go off screen. Move them backwards frame by frame, so it looks like the puppet is moving forwards. You can use the two sleeves to wind the front and back of your puppet to different heights, and change its angle to add extra movement.

HANDY TIP!

Move clouds and buildings at a steady rate. Moving a cloud by about half of its length per frame of animation is usually enough for capturing smooth motion.

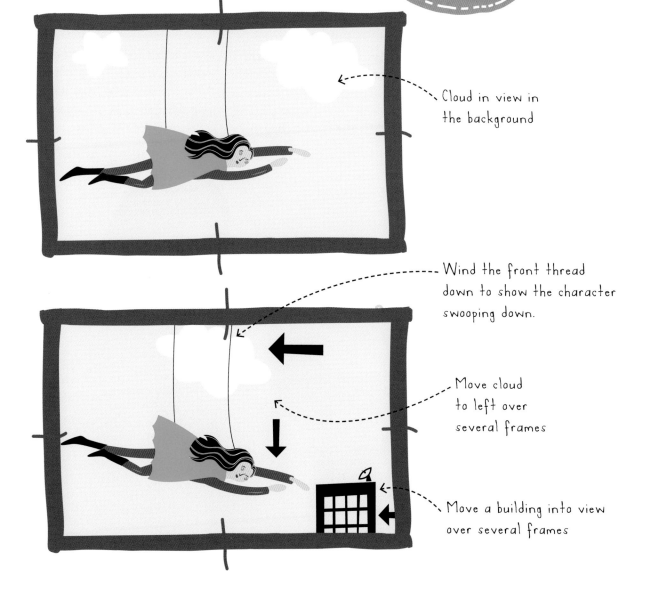

Cloud in view in the background

Wind the front thread down to show the character swooping down.

Move cloud to left over several frames

Move a building into view over several frames

FILM IT LIKE A PRO

By now I hope you've had lots of fun making models, building sets and creating fantastic animated movement. The techniques you are already practising are the same as those used by Aardman Animations to create their brilliant cinematic masterpieces starring *Wallace & Gromit*, and by Henry Selick for *The Nightmare Before Christmas* and *Coraline*. In this chapter, you'll learn how to make your animations look professional; you'll discover the methods animators use to make their creations more real and exciting.

Tip 1: DRAMATIC LIGHTING

If you want lighting that adds atmosphere to your animation, light your set with a desk lamp and turn off all other lights in the room. Point the desk lamp at your set from one side at a low angle. This will attach a strong shadow to everything in the scene, creating a moody feel.

Lights can get hot very quickly, so be careful where you stand your lamp. If possible, use an LED lamp as it stays much cooler. Keep the lead of your lamp away from where you'll be moving about, to avoid accidentally knocking the light and shifting all the shadows.

HANDY TIP!
You can animate the light source, too! Move your light as you would a character, frame by frame. This makes the shadows move as you move the light. If you are moving a character at the same time, it introduces an exciting, mind-boggling effect.

Tip 2: LOSE THE SHADOWS

To avoid multiple shadows, make sure there aren't any other lights shining onto the set. And to soften the shadows, bounce the light from your desk lamp off a white surface (such as a piece of card) onto the set. This spreads the light and gives the scene a softer look. On professional sets, animators often mount sheets of scrap polystyrene on special stands to bounce the right level of light onto the set at the correct angle! You can also use a wall, low ceiling or the underside of a shelf.

'WOW' FACTOR!

TRY BOUNCING THE LIGHT OFF SOME COLOURED PAPER, AND YOU WILL GET COLOURED LIGHT BOUNCING BACK ONTO YOUR SET. YOU CAN EVEN INTRODUCE SOME CRAZY EFFECTS BY BOUNCING A SECOND LIGHT OFF A DIFFERENT COLOUR, OR HOW ABOUT SHINING LOTS OF LIGHTS, CREATING MULTIPLE SHADOWS IN DIFFERENT SHADES OF COLOUR? TRY IT AND SEE WHAT HAPPENS!

Tip 3: AVOIDING FLICKER

A flickering image is the enemy of any camera-based animation. Most often this is caused by failing to control the lighting, such as ignoring the subtle changes in daylight during shooting or from people opening doors, moving around and casting their shadows on the set. Don't let your shadow fall across the set and don't wear a white top that reflects light back onto the set.

USING YOUR CAMERA

We've introduced you to some of the basics of setting up your camera. Here are some more advanced tricks of the trade that will help you improve your camerawork. They will need lots of practice and patience before you master them, but the effort will be worthwhile.

Tip 1: CAMERA MOVES

The 'camera move' is a technique where you move the camera frame by frame rather than animating a character or an object. This allows you to follow a character or reveal a part of the set that had been out of view. Animated camera moves are tricky to film, because a tiny move from the camera makes a huge difference on the screen. But if you can pull it off, the effect will blow your mind!

The same rules apply as with all animated movement – Keep the moves evenly spaced between frames and stay true to a line of movement. You will need a big set, too, to pull off a camera move, so that you can rotate the camera around without it catching anything beyond the edge of your set.

HANDY TIP!
Consider buying a mini-tripod on which to mount your smartphone or camera, rather than relying on a blob of modelling clay. There are several types to choose from – I like the bendy ones best!

HANDY TIP!
Don't let the edge of the set appear in your screen, either in a camera move or from a careless set-up. It will break the magic of your animation. Nothing ruins the believability of your piece more than spotting someone doing the washing up beyond the edge of the sky!

Tip 2: FOLLOWING THE PUPPET

It's sometimes better to take a more rough-and-ready approach to filming. In this method you follow a vehicle or character with the camera. You keep them in the centre of the image, using onion skinning to line up each live image with the previous frame. This means you move the camera but your eyes remain focused on the vehicle or character, and so action is less confusing for your audience.

You might have tried this approach when you were making a skateboarding pixilation. With a toy you have more control over the movement. Move the toy first, then gently move the camera a tiny amount. Use the ghost image on the onion skin to see when you have moved the camera enough to line up with the live image. Everything else will appear to have moved slightly backwards while the toy will remain in the same place on screen. Move everything a tiny bit at a time. Making tiny changes each time, sustain the camera move for at least five frames so that your animation captures a smooth sliding or rotating motion rather than a sudden jolt.

'WOW' FACTOR!

TRY RECREATING THE 'PAUSED ACTION' EFFECT DEVELOPED BY ARTIST TIM MACMILLAN THAT WAS FAMOUSLY USED IN THE FILM *THE MATRIX*. PAUSE AT THE MOST DRAMATIC POINT OF AN ACTION – A PUPPET IN THE MIDDLE OF A JUMP, FOR EXAMPLE. THEN MOVE THE CAMERA AROUND IT IN AN ARC, KEEPING THE PUPPET IN THE SAME PLACE ON SCREEN USING THE ONION SKIN.

FANTASTIC WORLDS

Every animated film has its own look, its own logic and follows its own set of rules. You can think of this as the world of your film. This means that as long as you stay faithful to the world, you're free to build fantastical sets full of detail, or make a rough set with objects you have found around the house.

WHAT'S YOUR WORLD LIKE?

If you have a hobby you want to describe, a funny story to tell or a favourite period of history you wish to bring to life, you can use them as inspirations for your animations. But remember to keep the world of your animation consistent. For example, in a silly, comic world, it might make perfect sense that a real hand comes in and squishes your main character., whereas such an action in a realistic setting is likely to break the illusion.

HANDY TIP!

A few shaped strips of coloured card can be propped up to make layers of hills and mountains or the waves in the sea. Mount your camera low so you are not able to see the floor of the set in between them. Now you can put a boat, a swimmer or a giant whale in the gaps between the waves, and they will appear to be in the water.

'WOW' FACTOR!

A CAMERA CAPTURES A 2D IMAGE SO CAN'T TELL WHAT IS CLOSE AND WHAT IS FAR AWAY. TRY LINING UP A NEARBY TOY OR A MODELLING CLAY PUPPET WITH A REAL HUMAN WHO IS STANDING FAR AWAY. HEY PRESTO – AN INSTANT SHRINKING EFFECT! USING THIS TECHNIQUE, YOU CAN 'HIGH FIVE' AN ACTION FIGURE OR COME FACE TO FACE WITH A TOY RABBIT!

ALWAYS "BUILD TO CAMERA"

As you build your set, always look at what your camera will be seeing. That way you will see if the details will be hidden behind other objects or be too small to be picked out by the camera, before spending lots of time on them. This is known as 'building to camera'.

I once spent a day making tiny fruits and vegetables for a shop window. In the final film, the audience could only see them as out-of-focus blobs of colour. If I'd 'built to camera', I would have realised early on that I could have just scribbled them on a piece of paper for the same effect! Having said that, don't be afraid of adding tiny details if they can be seen – after all, it is the details that make people really believe in the world you have created.

SOUND EFFECTS

Sound is an important part of any animation. Even in the early days of cinema, 'silent' films were usually accompanied by soundtracks, performed live by musicians in the theatre.

Your animation app often features simple sound effects and longer audio clips that you can add as you animate. Check out the app's help guides online and search for 'audio features'. To add more complicated sounds, take a look at Super Skill 10: Putting It All Together.

SHOOT FROM ABOVE

There is a whole different area of stop motion we have yet to explore! There is a special technique to make two-dimensional animation using the stop motion techniques you have been learning so far. You position the camera above your stage and make the action happen in the flat world you create beneath it.

CUT-OUT ANIMATION

On pages 6–9 you made a flickbook, which is a form of 2D (two-dimensional) animation. Another kind of 2D animation is cut-out animation. By laying out cut-out paper puppets on a flat surface and filming from above, animators are free from the restrictions of gravity. They can make their characters leap, fly and balance on one leg without the need for a flying rig!

You tried some cut-out animation when you created explosions. You can use the same technique to animate figures made from coloured paper and images cut from magazines. You'll make your scene flat on the table, with the camera looking straight down upon it.

'WOW' FACTOR!

THE 'SHOOT FROM ABOVE' TECHNIQUE WAS USED BY TERRY GILLIAM TO MAKE HIS FAMOUS ANIMATIONS FOR *MONTY PYTHON*, AND BY RUSSIAN ANIMATION MASTER YURI NORSTEIN TO MAKE HIS CHILDREN'S TALE *HEDGEHOG IN THE FOG*. LOTTE REINIGER USED THE SAME METHOD TO MAKE HER FAMOUS FAIRYTALE SILHOUETTE FILM *THE ADVENTURES OF PRINCE ACHMED* IN THE 1920s.

HANDY TIP!

Don't feel limited to flat card, just because you are shooting from above. See what things are lying about the house that could be used in your setting. A small plastic fork could make an unusual arm or a pair of buttons might make eyes. Remember to ask if you can borrow things.

How To Make The Set

WHAT YOU NEED:

- A2 sheet of card as background
- Mixed colours of A4 paper
- Scissors
- Paper glue
- Your box studio (see page 29)
- Cardboard lid for your box studio

You make your set using a method called collage. Collage involves creating one big image by gluing together a collection of other images and objects, in a different order.

MAKE IT BIG

Use an A2 sheet of paper as your background, so there is plenty of space for the action to unfold.

KEEP IT SIMPLE

For your first attempt, make a plain background so that you will be able to see your characters clearly on top of it.

STICK IT DOWN

Stick the background elements down firmly really well, so you don't knock them out of position when you are moving characters.

PLAN AHEAD

Plan out your action before you begin. For example, if your story needs an open doorway, cut it out before you start animating.

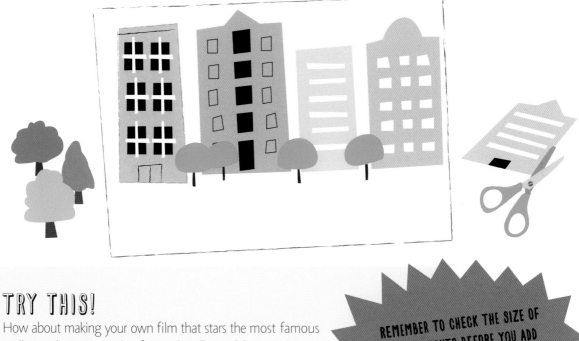

TRY THIS!

How about making your own film that stars the most famous Hollywood actors or pokes fun at the silliest celebrities? Cut out pictures of them from magazines to use as figures. You can also add your own speech bubbles to the scene.

REMEMBER TO CHECK THE SIZE OF YOUR CUTOUTS BEFORE YOU ADD ANY DETAIL BY PUTTING THEM IN FRONT OF THE CAMERA TO SEE HOW THEY FIT ON SCREEN.

NOW FOR FIGURES!

Now it's time to make your flat characters move across the flat set. Just as you did with your claymation puppet, you can make separate arms, legs, body and head. Once you've made your characters, you'll be ready to animate some amazing movement!

Making Characters

I like to keep my characters' bodies quite simple, using basic cut-out shapes. The character shown here is about 15 centimetres tall and made from two different colours of card.

Make three different leg shapes: one bent leg, one leg with the foot angled so it's leaning forwards, and one leg leaning slightly back.

HANDY TIP!
People often use paper fasteners to fix limbs to bodies, but they don't work very well for animation. Instead, a pinch of sticky tack will stop limbs moving by accident, and makes it possible to swap one shape for another.

You can move the legs in the sequence shown here to make the character walk.

Curved rectangles are best for arms and legs that are bent.

Making Faces

You can bring out the personalities of your characters by adding detail to their faces. Make a simple face shape and cut out several types of eyes, noses and mouths, then begin mixing and matching to animate different expressions.

HANDY TIP!
Make the whites of the eyes and the coloured parts (the irises) separately. That way you can make the eyes look up, down, left and right. It's amazing how much character eye movement can give to your model.

You can also cut out the heads of TV celebrities, sportspeople or film stars from magazines. If you can find multiple images of the same celebrity's head, try swapping them between frames, to give them a variety of expressions.

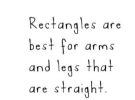

Rectangles are best for arms and legs that are straight.

HANDY TIP!
Swapping shapes is the key to making complex moves with ease. It would be really hard to animate a fist becoming an open hand if you tried to make the fingers separately. If you just swap hand shapes, so frame one is a fist and frame two is an open hand, it becomes super simple.

TIME FOR THE CAMERA!

So now you have your set and characters, but how do you hold your camera over the flat collage? You build a shelf for it, of course! Here's how to make a shelf to fit inside your box studio. It's a tricky task even for those with super-duper craft skills, so make this only if you enjoy the challenge of building things. Or ask an adult to help you.

HANDY TIP!

If you haven't made the box studio from Super Skill 5, there are other ways to hold your camera steady over a flat set. You could tape your device so it looks over the edge of a table, or use a stool that has a hole in the seat! Improvisation is a big part of animation!

WHAT YOU NEED:

- Corrugated cardboard, available at many supermarkets and big DIY stores
- Ruler or measuring tape
- Pencil
- Scissors or craft knife
- Strong double-sided tape
- Flexible desk lamp

Step 1

Make the stand by referring to the template in the illustration below. You will need three measurements: the length of the inside of your studio box from front to back, the width of the box and the height your camera device needs to be to see most of the bottom of the box.

1 Hold your device where you can see the whole artwork on the side of the box, and mark the height.

2 Mark out a big piece of corrugated cardboard to the right size.

3 Lightly score where your folds should be (see image below) with rounded craft scissors or the edge of a plastic ruler, to make a nice clean fold.

4 Check that your folded stand fits snuggly in your studio box (see Step 3 on the next page), and make any necessary adjustments.

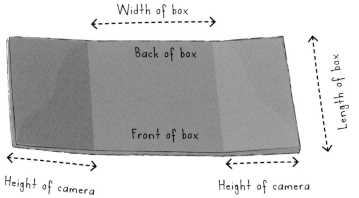

Width of box

Back of box

Length of box

Front of box

Height of camera

Height of camera

Step 2

Next, you need to fit your camera device to the stand.

1 Make a hole big enough for your camera lens to see through.

2 Cut a new piece of card the same size as the stand top. You might need to ask an adult to help you.

3 Trace the outline of your device in the centre of the new card and cut out a hole so the lens lines up with that in the stand.

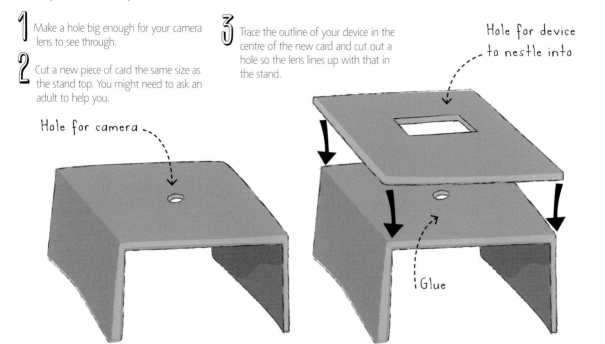

Hole for device to nestle into

Hole for camera

Glue

Step 3

Finally, place the camera stand on top of the studio box and add lighting. Now you're ready to animate!

1 Slot the stand into the box and add your set.

2 Use a flexible desk lamp to light the set.

Device

HANDY TIP!
Don't stand your lamp too close or you will get bleached-out patches in your animation. To even out the light, put a sheet of white paper or slightly crinkled silver foil at the back of the box and shine the lamp onto that.

Background and characters

FURTHER ADVENTURES IN 2D

Now it's time to try whiteboard and sand animation, which are both 2D animation techniques. They both involve adding and taking away marks to create movement, but each technique achieves a different look. Whiteboard animation is very sharp and clear, whereas sand animation is soft with a dreamy quality.

WHITEBOARD ANIMATION

Whiteboard animation is among the quickest and least fussy ways to animate. Check out the popular film *Minilogue – Hitchhiker's Choice* online or type 'whiteboard animation' into a search engine and you'll come across some inspirational examples.

A common mistake in whiteboard animation is completing a movement in too few frames and ending up with animation that jumps from the start to the end of the action, with little movement in between. Be patient as you draw your frames. Focus on creating a flowing motion rather than the finished drawing.

WHAT YOU NEED:

- A whiteboard – anything from A4 to A2 size (If you do not a have whiteboard, use a wipe-clean surface that will fit in the bottom of your studio box)
- Whiteboard marker
- Tissue or wet wipes

HANDY TIP!
Work slowly and methodically. It's easy to focus too much on the drawing and then forget to click the capture button!

Try it out

Let's start with a quick experiment to learn how the technique works. You should end up with a mark that travels across the screen and then branches out and splits into two marks. Once you're confident, you can try out some ideas of your own.

○ Make a mark on the whiteboard, just a few centimetres long and capture the frame.

○ Wipe away the tail end of the mark with a wet wipe, tissue or your finger. Make the changes quite small until you become used to the speed of it.

○ Use onion skinning to see how much you have wiped away and added, so you can keep track of how much the image has changed since the last frame you captured.

○ Keep adding to front end of the mark and taking away from the tail. You can make the mark grow by adding more than you take away, and shrink it again by taking away more than you add.

'WOW' FACTOR!

USE DIFFERENT COLOURED PENS TO CREATE A RANGE OF EFFECTS. TRY TO INTRODUCE MEANING TO THE DIFFERENT COLOURS – FOR EXAMPLE, YOU COULD TURN YOUR ANIMATION INTO A DANCE OR A FIGHT BETWEEN BLUE AND RED.

○ As you move the mark forwards, sometimes grow it longer and other times shrink it down. But don't switch too abruptly from growing to shrinking to growing again or you won't create a smooth flow of movement.

○ Add a branch to the mark, so as you wipe away the end, the mark splits into two.

○ See how many branches you can draw before you lose control of all the marks and their movements.

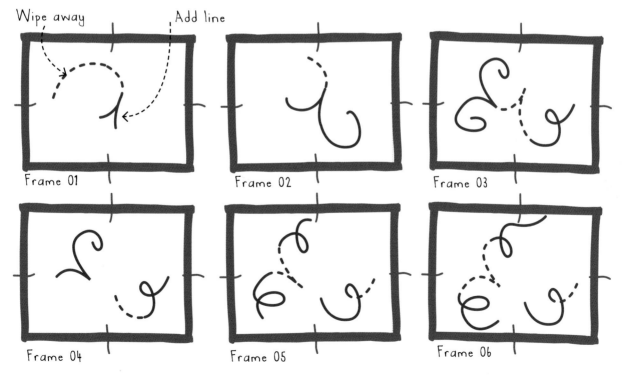

Wipe away   Add line

Frame 01   Frame 02   Frame 03

Frame 04   Frame 05   Frame 06

SAND ANIMATION

Sand animation is a soft and flowing form of animation. It is great for telling dreamy stories and making natural forms. This technique is used to great effect by the Canadian animator Caroline Leaf in a film called *The Owl Who Married a Goose*. It is a very sad story and definitely worth a watch. You can find a link for it on page 62.

SHINING LIGHT THROUGH SAND

For this animation technique you need a clear plastic box or tray to hold the sand, a light to shine beneath it and a way to hold your camera device steady above it. The sand in the bottom of the box blocks out the light. But when you make a mark in the sand, the light shines through, making the marked bit come out against the dark background.

You can make a cardboard stand, just like the one you made for your cut-out animation. If you don't want to make another stand, you can support your sand-filled box between two tables and have the lamp shine underneath it. Use a tripod to support your camera device above the sand.

WHAT YOU NEED:

- Corrugated cardboard
- Large clear plastic lunchbox
- Scissors
- Dry sand or flour
- Flexible desk lamp

THE SAND ANIMATION SET-UP

Make a sand-box stand like the device stand featured on pages 50 and 51. The sand box stand will sit underneath your device stand in your cardboard box studio, supporting a transparent lunchbox underneath your camera.

Device

Lunch box

Sand

HANDY TIP!
Flour gives a similar effect to sand but is slightly harder to control.

BE CAREFUL!
DO NOT TO LOOK DIRECTLY AT YOUR DESK LAMP, EVEN THROUGH THE SAND. ALWAYS SET THE LAMP TO ONE SIDE.

Try Different Tools

You can make marks in the sand using your fingers or cotton buds. If you are not using much sand, try sweeping it with a brush to form interesting shapes. It's a way of moving grains of sand around your tray for a unique effect.

Experiment With Sand

Start with no sand in your tray. Let sand flow from your palm, a little at a time, to create shapes that grow and spread from frame to frame.

Use Stencils

You can create simple characters with sand by using stencils. Cut your character's shape out of a piece of card that is just a little bigger than the character itself. Put the card on your surface and pour sand into the hole. Carefully lift the card to leave the character shape formed in sand.

No sand

Sand

Areas thickly covered in sand will be dark, while space with little or no sand will be light.

WELL DONE!

You've nearly reached the end of the animation Super Skills. There is one more chapter about editing, but you have now learnt all the classic animation skills and know how to avoid common mistakes.

PUTTING IT ALL TOGETHER

Did you know that you don't have to edit shots together to make a film? You can just plan out your film and shoot each scene separately or tell the whole story from a single camera position. But editing can make your movie so much better and help you take out the mistakes. For example, you can cut away from a great shot of a killer robot just before your brother put his hand in shot and knocked it over. You can also use editing to switch scenes and add dramatic music… editing allows you to get really creative!

BUILDING IT UP

Once you have taken enough frames to produce some continuous movement, you've made a 'shot'. Put together a few shots and you have a 'scene'. Put the scenes together and start editing together your own short movie!

CHOOSING EDITING SOFTWARE

To edit your shots together, you need some basic editing software. This will allow you to work with whole shots, scenes and add effects such as music. Windows, Linux and Apple Mac computer operating systems have free software installed for editing home movies, and that's all you need. Look at the chart below to check what software to look for on your computer.

HANDY TIP!
Starting editing can be scary. Don't be afraid to ask an adult to help you. You'll definitely want to look at the online tutorials that are available for the particular software you'll be using.

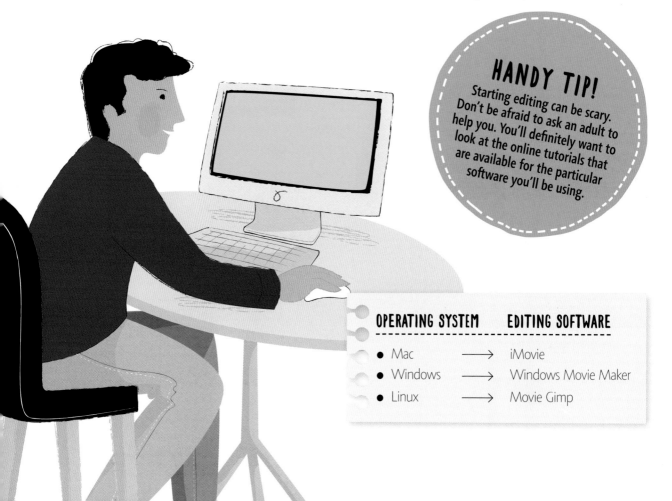

OPERATING SYSTEM		EDITING SOFTWARE
• Mac	⟶	iMovie
• Windows	⟶	Windows Movie Maker
• Linux	⟶	Movie Gimp

EXPORTING YOUR CLIPS

Before you edit your shots or clips together, you need to get them out of your animation software into a movie or file format that your editing software will understand. Your app has a 'Share' or 'Export' button for making a version of the film that works outside the app. You have the option to publish straight to a site such as YouTube, but if you want to put more than one movie file together you'll need to Export or Share them to your device's 'Camera Roll' or 'Video Library' or 'iTunes'.

Once you have exported your shots or clips to one of those locations, you can plug your device into your computer and upload them to your hard drive. It's a good idea to create one folder where you keep all the files that make up your film.

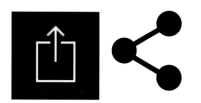

These are typical icons for 'Export' and 'Share'.

When you open your animation app's Export or Share screen, you should find icons that lead directly to websites where you can share your animation.

HANDY TIP!

Animation professionals are very careful about keeping files organised. They often have a project folder for each film, a separate folder inside that for each scene, and another folder for audio. They also give each movie file a clearly identifiable shot number or name.

DIGITAL FILES

Each animation project you have shot will become a 'movie file', 'movie clip' or 'video file' when you export it. Those are all names for the same thing – a digital file containing moving images. Most apps will only export a movie file format called 'Mp4', which works in most editing software.

FEATURES OF EDITING SOFTWARE

You will find that different editing programs have their own way of showing the same features. If only things were simple! But fear not! They all work on the same principle and have the same basic elements.

THE PROJECT WINDOW

One of the main areas of your software contains the files that make up the movie – your shots. Sometimes this window is labelled "Media", sometimes it's called the "Project window", "Assets", or "Events" or "Clip bin". You can import movie files into this window by dragging the files onto it from where they are stored on your computer. If this doesn't work, use the "File > Import" menu.

THE TIMELINE

You also have a "Timeline", which is the area where you put the shots together, one after the other like words in a sentence. You drag your files into the timeline. You will be familiar with a timeline from your stop motion software. But, don't forget, in the editing software timeline, you are dealing with movie clips, not individual frames.

Sometimes the editing timeline is an empty line that runs along the bottom of the screen. Other times it is more like the lines in a book, running from left to right and one on top of the other, becoming longer as you add to it.

THE VIEWING WINDOW

As you add shots to your timeline, you will be able to watch your work in progress in a 'Viewing window'. This is often the largest panel on the screen.

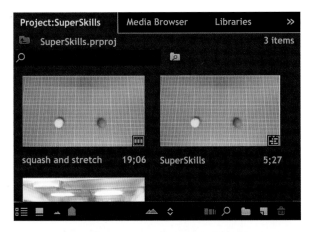

The 'Project' panel and the 'Timeline' panel from a software program called *Adobe Premiere*.

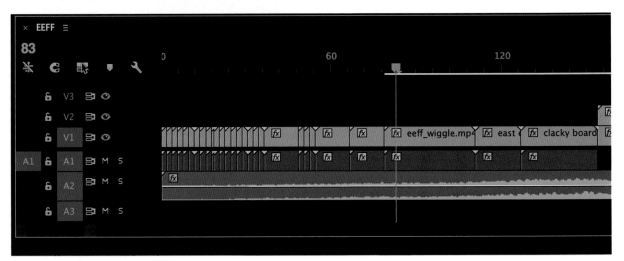

A typical editing software screen

AUDIO

'Audio', or sound, usually sits in a separate line in the timeline, underneath the video. Most editing software will come with a large library of sound effects and free-to-use music loops. You can add to these by recording your own sound effects or by visiting online sound libraries (see page 62 for some links).

ATMOS

There is a useful idea in sound design called 'Atmosphere', or 'Atmos' for short. It refers to the general sounds we're usually unaware of that make up the character of any space, like the hum of distant traffic, birds singing or people muttering.

It's a good term to know when you're searching in the sound effects library of your software. Try starting with this sort of background sound, dragging it into position under part of your animation. You can then add shorter sound effects, such as the crashes and bangs of the action on top of the atmosphere sounds. This layering of sounds will make your animation sound more real.

THERE IS NEVER REALLY SILENCE, ANYWHERE IN THE WORLD. EVEN IN THE QUIETEST PLACE YOU WILL BE ABLE TO HEAR THE SOUNDS OF YOUR BREATHING AND YOUR HEARTBEAT!

EDITING YOUR ANIMATIONS

Every software has its own way of doing things, so in these pages we've provided a general guide. The most useful advice when it comes to editing is to be organised, take your time and back up your original files.

Step 1: BRINGING YOUR SHOTS TOGETHER

Once your files are organised into one project folder on your computer, change the names and number them so it's easy to find in which order they should appear.

Some software copies a movie into the project, so it is stored inside the project, whatever happens to the original file. Other software relies on the movie being where it was before you dragged it in, and having the same name. In either case, it's good to put everything into one folder and save the project there, too.

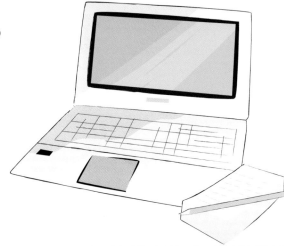

Step 2: OPEN YOUR EDITING SOFTWARE

Drag your files to the Project window, or go to File › Import Movie. Now you can drag them across to the Timeline, dropping them into it in the correct order.

If you have a storyboard, you can tick off shots as you add them to the Timeline. You have now created the 'rough cut' edit of your masterpiece! Well done! Watch the play back and take a break.

Step 3: EDITING CLIPS

You can adjust the speed of your clip, usually by right clicking on it and going to 'Speed/Duration' or by using a slider. Changing the speed to 200% will make it run twice as fast, changing it to 50% will make it run at half speed.

If you hover over the end of a clip, you can drag the end, or 'out point', shorter, to cut off the end of the clip. This

is useful if something spoiled the end of the shot or if you shot more at the end than you need.

If you need to cut in the middle of your clip, use the razor blade tool. You might want to do this if there is a stray hand in shot or to insert a different shot into the scene.

TRANSITIONS

There will be lots of weird transitions on offer. A transition is the change from one scene to another. So you can have one clip wiping across the screen to the next one, or becoming a star shape or a rotating cube. Use transitions to represent things you cannot animate easily, for example, to show time has passed or that you are travelling far away.

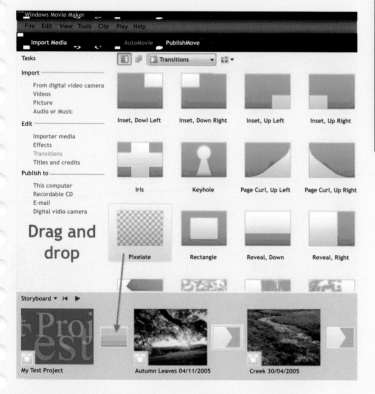

HANDY TIP!

Use transitions sparingly because too many can interrupt the flow of your story.

Step 4: TITLES & CREDITS!

To name your film, click on 'Titles' or 'Text' and change the text from 'Title' to the name of your film. Drag it to the start of the film. Do the same at the end of the film but fill in 'Directed and Animated by' with your name! Don't forget to credit anyone who helped you.

NOW THAT YOU'VE PRACTISED ALL THE SKILLS, YOU ARE OFFICIALLY AN ANIMATOR AND WORTHY OF WEARING A SHIRT WITH THE MOTTO "THE MAGIC LIVES BETWEEN THE FRAMES". KEEP ENJOYING THE PROCESS. SEE YOU LATER, ANIMATOR!

USEFUL LINKS

There are lots of great resources online for animators, and hundreds of animations made by first time animators are uploaded every day. Here are some great animations you can watch online to discover more about the animation process, as well as a selection of useful online resources.

ANIMATIONS

'The Owl Who Married a Goose'
www.nfb.ca/film/owl_who_married_goose
This short animation by Caroline Leaf is based on an Inuit legend. Watch it to learn more about the effects that are possible using sand animation techniques.

'Minilogue – Hitchhiker's Choice'
vimeo.com/158803
This short film is a great example of what you can create using whiteboard animation.

'Her Morning Elegance'
vimeo.com/13781225
This music video by Oren Lavie has been made using stop motion photography. By using small movements and taking many frames, the animators have created the impression that the actress is walking and swimming.

Rex the Dog: 'Bubblicious'
www.youtube.com/watch?v=acay3S2PhSg
This music video was made using stop motion and replacement animation. It's really fun to watch and shows you how the 3D characters were made during the film.

USEFUL RESOURCES

www.stopmotionanimation.com
As you get more advanced in Stop-Motion animation, you might find it useful to visit this website. There is a huge amount of information and advice from stop motion supergeeks. It can be overwhelming, but there is also a 'Handbook' section that gives newbies a great place to start.

www.sounddogs.com
Sounddogs is a commercial online library of sound effects. Explore the site to see what sounds are available.

www.aardman.com
Aardman is a fantastic stop-motion studio based in Bristol in the UK. They make series and features such as *Wallace and Grommit*, *Morph*, and *Shaun the Sheep* and are famous throughout the world for their claymation work. Their website has clips and info galore.

brickfilms.com
A great way to start making toy animations is with LEGO bricks and other construction toys. Brickfilms is the oldest website hosting films and sharing advice between users. Take a look at the films its members have made. If they inspire you to make your own, you could submit it to the site!

Website information is correct at time of going to press. The publishers cannot accept liability for any information or links found on third-party websites.

GLOSSARY

2D two-dimensional = flat

3D three-dimensional = lumpy! Model animators are sometimes called lumpies by computer animators, a badge that model animators wear with honour.

ATMOS atmosphere. The general sounds heard in a space

AUDIO sound

CLAYMATION animation created frame by frame using changes made to modelling clay.

CLIP short piece of animation

COLLAGE image made by cutting out other images and gluing them, and sometimes other objects, together in a different order

EDITING assembling and making changes to something

FILE format particular and mysterious way a computer has encoded information

FLYING RIG support structure that allows a puppet to fly

FRAME single still image that is, or will be, part of an animated sequence

FRAME RATE speed in frames per second (fps) that the images in an animation will be played back to you

MOVIE moving image

MOVIE FORMAT particular and mysterious way a computer has encoded the visual information contained in your animation

ONION SKINNING semi-transparent, ghostly image of the last frame you shot, overlaid onto whatever is in front of the camera now

PIXEL tiny square of colour that is used, in their millions, by digital displays to show images

PIXILATION animating the human form; from the same root word as pixie, meaning magic

REPLACEMENT ANIMATION swapping one object with a very similar object to fool the eye into thinking it's the same object that has changed shape

RESOLUTION either the end of a story; or the size of a digital image, usually measured in pixels

SCENE everything in a film that happens during one situation, before the set or scenery changes

SHOT everything in a film that happens between the start and end of a sequence of images that are similar enough to give the illusion of one movement

STOP MOTION animation created by the moving of inanimate objects

TIMELINE visual way of showing how clips or images are spread out over time by laying them out in a line

TRANSITION pre-programmed video effect that changes how one clip changes or cuts to the next

VIDEO digital moving image

INDEX